D1327446

AERIAL GUNNERS OF WORLD WAR II

by Elbert M. Hoppenstedt

Perfection Learning®

Cover Design: Mike Aspengren
Inside Design: Mark Hagenberg

About the Author

Elbert Hoppenstedt is a retired teacher, principal, and school superintendent. During World War II, he was stationed in Italy with the Fifteenth Air Force. While teaching, he published six mysteries for children.

Currently, Mr. Hoppenstedt resides in sunny Florida, where he spends his time writing, gardening, and taking frequent cruises.

Image Credits:

Mike Aspengren: cover; AP/Wide World Photos: pp. 37, 42, 63; www.bellsaviation.com by GM Bell: pp. 12, 13, 45; © Bettmann/CORBIS: pp. 22, 34, 35; © Jeff Albertson/CORBIS: p. 27; Tony Manninen: p. 24

Clipart.com: pp. 4, 6, 8, 11, 15, 19, 20, 41; Corel: pp. 5 (bottom), 9, 18, 31, 59, 60; Digital Stock: p. 38; NARA: pp. 5 (top), 10, 14, 25, 28, 29, 47, 49, 50, 52, 55, 56, 58, 61, 64, 65; Photos.com: pp. 7, 16, 21, 23, 32, 54, 66; Perfection Learning: p. 39

Printed in the United States of America. For information, contact

Perfection Learning® Corporation
1000 North Second Avenue,
P.O. Box 500, Logan, Iowa 51546-0500.
Tel: 1-800-831-4190 • Fax: 1-800-543-2745
perfectionlearning.com

1 2 3 4 5 6 PP 09 08 07 06 05 04

Paperback ISBN 0-7891-6225-3
Cover Craft® ISBN 0-7569-1909-6

CONTENTS

CHAPTER 1

GETTING READY FOR THE MISSION

U.S. Army Air Force Base
Grottaglie, Italy
January 1944

It's 5:30 in the morning and still dark outside. Two hundred and fifty young men are in the **mess hall** having breakfast. They've been out of the **sack** since 4:30. That's when the operations sergeant made the rounds. He woke up everyone whose name was posted on the assignment sheet the night before.

Right now, the men are very quiet. They are all thinking the same thing. "Will my plane get back safely? Will I be alive tonight?"

Most of these airmen are teenagers. They **enlisted** soon after the Japanese bombed Pearl Harbor. Some were still in high school.

Pearl Harbor

PEARL HARBOR

On a quiet Sunday morning, December 7, 1941, the Japanese attacked the Pearl Harbor Naval Base in Hawaii. The surprise attack killed 2400 Americans and destroyed or badly damaged 18 ships and 200 airplanes.

The next day, President Franklin D. Roosevelt addressed the nation over the radio. He announced that the United States had declared war on Japan. Three days later, the United States also declared war on Germany and Italy.

President Roosevelt signing the declaration of war

When these men enlisted, they were children. Now, ten months later, they are men. They've experienced war. They've faced death time and time again.

Each time the B-24 and B-17 bombers take off, some don't come back. These men know the facts. The odds are 60 percent that they'll never fly the required number of **sorties**. That's why airmen receive extra pay. That's why they've all been given the rank of sergeant.

B-17 bomber taking off

ARMY MILITARY RANKS

These are the ranks, from low to high, of the men in the army who were not officers.

private
private first class
corporal
sergeant
staff sergeant
technical sergeant
master sergeant

They are the tail gunners, the ball-**turret** gunners, the waist gunners, the top-turret gunners, and the nose gunners. They are all enlisted men—staff and technical sergeants.

The men eat their powdered eggs and toast and drink their coffee. A few words pass between them.

"I hope it's not the Ploesti oil fields again," one man says.

PLOESTI OIL FIELDS

The Ploesti oil fields and refinery in Romania supplied more than 30 percent of the petroleum used by Germany in its war efforts. On August 1, 1943, U.S. bombing raids began. In no time, the oil fields were on fire, and Germany had to look elsewhere for fuel.

U.S. bombers flying over the Ploesti oil fields

"Better not be. Half the men didn't make it back last time," another answers.

"Maybe it will be a **milk run**."

"I hope so."

Breakfast is over, and the men climb into a waiting truck. They're already dressed for the mission in electrically heated undergarments and fleece-lined leather boots, pants, and jackets.

The men dressed as soon as they got up. They put on their **dog tags** and **GI** watches. They placed their wallets in secret places under their mattresses. They took one last look at the letters they'd written to family and friends back home in case they didn't come back.

The trucks carry the men to the Group Operations Room. All the men are checked at the door. No **unauthorized** person is allowed to enter the **briefing** room. What is about to take place is considered **classified**.

Once inside, the men seat themselves on makeshift plank seats placed across several concrete blocks. Attendance is taken. Members of each of the crews are called off. Finally a staff officer announces that all men are present and accounted for.

ARMY MILITARY RANKS

These are the ranks, from low to high, of the army officers.

second lieutenant
lieutenant
captain
major
lieutenant colonel
colonel
brigadier general
major general
lieutenant general
general
general of the army

A colonel enters the room. All the men stand at **attention**. The officer motions for the men to be seated. His aide pulls back a curtain to show a large map of the entire European theater of operations.

European theater in 1944

EUROPEAN THEATER OF OPERATIONS

During World War II, the United States fought in theaters of operations—the Pacific theater and the European theater. The Pacific theater took place on the Pacific Ocean and on many of its islands. It was here that the United States fought the Japanese. The war with Germany and Italy was fought on the continents of Europe and Africa, or the European theater.

Drawn across the map is a line showing the route of the day's mission. At the end of the line sits the target. Groans sound from all corners of the room. The planes are headed to Vienna, Austria. It won't be a milk run today!

Vienna is a heavily defended city. Antiaircraft **emplacements** are on every side. ME-109s patrol the skies. The men don't even get a fighter **escort** because Vienna is so far away. The fighters don't carry enough fuel to fly the round-trip.

ME-109

The ME-109 was the best known and most widely produced German fighter of World War II. It was the backbone of the German fighter command and ruled the skies over Europe from 1939 to 1941. The ME-109s earned the respect of the Allies and were greatly feared by Allied bomber crews during the latter half of the war.

Allied war leaders: Winston Churchill (Britain), Franklin D. Roosevelt (United States), and Joseph Stalin (Russia)

ALLIES AND AXIS POWERS

Between 1939 and 1945, 46 countries joined the United States, England, and Russia to form the Allies. Seven countries formed the Axis nations—Germany, Italy, Japan, Bulgaria, Finland, Hungary, and Romania.

The colonel points out where the antiaircraft guns are positioned. He illustrates how the bomb run will be made. "I'll be in the lead plane," he says. "If anything should happen to me, Major Perkins in the *Gray Goose* will take command."

Next the weather officer speaks. He tells the crews that they will have heavy cloud cover at 15,000 feet as they cross over the Alps. "But the target area should be clear," he says. "There may be clouds at about 2000 feet here at the field by the time you get back," he adds. "I'll explain landing procedures during the officers' briefing."

Next, the operations officer describes the target the men are going after. A photographic view of the area is displayed on a screen.

German munitions dump exploding

"The primary targets are major German **munitions dumps** located in three buildings—here, here, and here," he says, pointing to three small squares. "Over here is the secondary target should you miss the primary one. These are **marshaling yards**. Intelligence tells us that there may be as many as 12 train cars carrying munitions waiting to be unloaded."

There is one last check before the men are dismissed. They must set their watches. At a signal from the colonel, the men pull out the stems of their watches and set the hour, minute, and second hands to the time he calls out. It is important that everyone has the exact time.

The briefing's over. The enlisted men file out of the operations room as the officers enter. The men climb into another waiting truck. It carries them to the supply building. There they pass a row of tables holding the equipment they will need.

AIRMEN'S EQUIPMENT

- Mae Wests are life jackets in case the planes **ditch** in the water.
- **Flak** vests are filled with chunks of metal. They can **deflect** any small pieces of flak that pierce a plane's **fuselage**.
- Fleece-lined helmets have built-in headsets that plug into a plane's intercom systems.
- Oxygen masks are needed at 20,000 feet. At that **altitude**, the air is so thin no one can live longer than a minute or two.
- Chest parachutes are needed in case the men have to **bail out**.

"If it doesn't work, bring it back. I'll issue you a new one," the private behind the table says as he hands out the parachutes. The men say nothing. They've heard the joke so often it's no longer funny. In fact, it hurts.

It's now time for the last part of the preparation—transportation to the flight line. Some men choose to walk, their parachutes slung over their backs. Others ride on a weapons carrier or truck.

www.bellsaviation.com

Chest parachute and harness

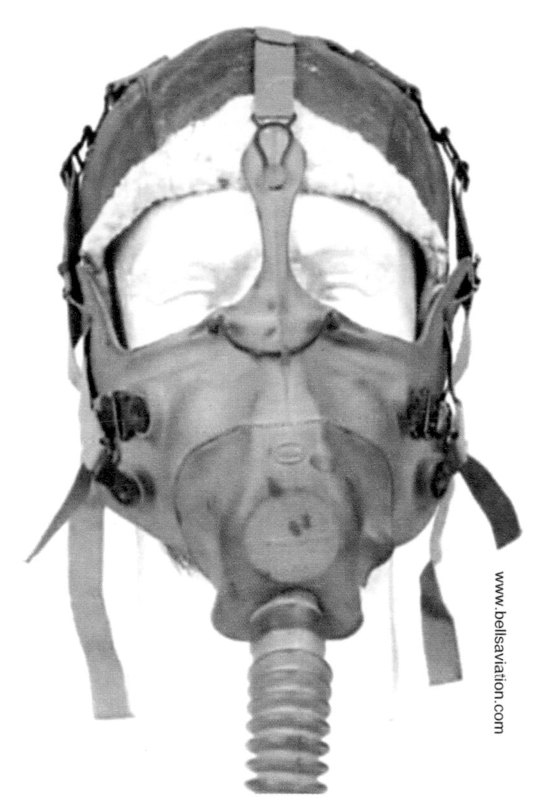
www.bellsaviation.com

B-5 flight helmet with A-10 oxygen mask

When they reach their planes, the men drop their loads on the **hardstand**. Some use their parachutes as pillows and drop off for a quick nap. Others stand in small groups discussing the day's mission.

Finally the jeep carrying the officers arrives. The enlisted men get up and head for their planes. It's time to begin the mission.

CHAPTER 2

THE BEST-TRAINED GUNNERS IN THE WORLD

From day one of enlistment until the day they flew overseas to begin combat, army enlistees went through a **rigorous** training program—seven days a week, eight to ten hours a day.

WOMEN IN WWII

During World War II, unmarried women were permitted to join the armed forces. Most of the women worked in military offices, freeing thousands of men to enter combat. Some women flew airplanes between U.S. military bases, delivering cargo. Male pilots could then fly in combat. The army sent many women overseas, but they were never part of the combat forces. Women in the navy and marines were not sent overseas. For this reason, male nouns and pronouns are used in this book when referring to the gunners and other officers and enlistees.

Nancy Harkness Love, director of the U.S. Women's Auxillary Ferry Squadron

Rope-climbing obstacle course used during basic training

Basic Training

The first phase was basic training where civilians became soldiers. They were taught how to salute properly. They learned how to make up a bed so the inspecting officer could bounce a coin on it. The men also learned how to march and do **close-order drill**.

At this stage in training, no assignment had yet been made as to which branch of the army they would be assigned—the air force or the infantry.

THE ARMED FORCES

At the time of WWII, the armed forces was made up of the army, the navy, the marines, and the Coast Guard. The Coast Guard became a special attachment of the navy during the war. The air force at that time was part of the army. It did not become an independent branch of the armed forces until 1947.

The only way a person could choose a branch of the service was to volunteer rather than be **drafted**. Volunteering only guaranteed the service branch, not a particular job.

After basic training, servicemen who showed high intelligence on I.Q. tests were then given further tests. These tests determined the job they were best suited for. They might be sent to gunnery school, to radio-operator school, or to flight-engineer school. They might qualify for the officers' flight-training program as navigators, bombardiers, or pilots.

Radio signaler

Radio-Operator Training

After leaving basic training, the soldiers chosen to become radio operators spent about six to eight weeks learning the fundamentals of radio. They learned how to repair transmitters and receivers. They had hands-on training installing antennas.

When they finished that part of their training, they attended classes to learn how to send and receive Morse code. For eight hours, these soldiers sat at booths and **transcribed** prerecorded coded messages that came through the earphones they wore. For part of the eight-hour sessions, they practiced sending codes on instruments called *bugs*.

In the beginning, their pace was slow—3 or 4 words a minute. By the time the course ended, they could receive or send 15 to 20 words per minute.

Next, the future radio operators attended gunnery school. They practiced on rifle ranges, shooting clay pigeons. They fired at targets from moving trucks and from low-flying aircraft.

MORSE CODE

Morse code is a system of dots and dashes that represent letters and numbers. Each letter or number is made up of one or more dots and dashes. The dots and dashes are signals sent by radio transmitters or by signal lights.

Morse Code Alphabet

A	.–	N	–.	0	–––––
B	–...	O	–––	1	.––––
C	–.–.	P	.––.	2	..–––
D	–..	Q	––.–	3	...––
E	.	R	.–.	4	....–
F	..–.	S	...	5	.....
G	––.	T	–	6	–....
H	....	U	..–	7	––...
I	..	V	...–	8	–––..
J	.–––	W	.––	9	––––.
K	–.–	X	–..–		
L	.–..	Y	–.––		
M	––	Z	––..		

Flight-Engineer Training

Flight engineers were responsible for repairing any part of an aircraft while it was airborne. They made visual checks of the entire aircraft just before takeoffs. They helped the pilots and copilots during takeoffs and landings by reading aloud information from the instrument panel.

To learn all of this, they attended a hands-on engineering school. These soldiers specialized in one particular type of aircraft—P-51s, B-25s, B-24s, or B-17s. Models of these planes were available for them to work on. Instructors who had been trained by the companies that manufactured the aircraft supervised the trainees. When the men finished engineering school, they, like the radio operators, attended gunnery school.

B-25 just before landing

P-51 Mustangs in flight

Gunnery Training

Gunnery training was quick but thorough. The gunners received practice in mechanical trainers where they shot at enemy aircraft moving rapidly across a screen—much like today's video games.

Gunners learned to identify enemy planes. Photographs of enemy aircraft were flashed on a screen for several seconds. The gunners had to name them quickly.

After about six months of training, the men were finally ready to join the crews of B-24 Liberators or B-17 Flying Fortresses.

B-24 Liberator

CHAPTER 3

A JOB FOR EVERY MAN

The U.S. Army Air Force created manuals with job descriptions for each position on a B-17 or a B-24 bomber. During the war, these manuals were **restricted**. Once World War II was over, they were available to anyone who wished to read them.

The following job descriptions were written for the pilot's benefit, informing him of what he should expect from each of his crew members.

Pilot

Your assignment to this B-17 airplane means that you are no longer just a pilot. You are now an airplane commander with all the duties and responsibilities of a command post.

You are now flying a ten-man weapon. It is your airplane and your crew. You are responsible for the safety and **efficiency** of the crew at all times—not just when you are flying and fighting, but for 24 hours every day.

Your crew is made up of specialists. Each man is an expert at his job. But how well he does his job and how effectively he plays his part as a member of your team will depend on how well you play your own part as an airplane commander.

Copilot

Your copilot is your assistant. He will assist you during flight and take over in case of an emergency.

Always remember that the copilot is a fully trained pilot—just like yourself. He answers to you only because of your position as the aircraft commander. The B-17 is a lot of airplane. It's more than one pilot can handle alone over a long period of time. Therefore, you have been provided with a second pilot who will share the duties.

Treat your copilot as a brother pilot. Remember that the more skilled he becomes as a pilot, the more effectively he will be able to perform the duties of the second in command. Be sure that he is able to do his share of flying in the pilot's seat—on takeoffs, landings, and instrument flying. He must be able to fly the aircraft under all conditions as well as you would fly it yourself.

The Navigator

Your navigator's job is to direct your flight from departure to destination and return. He must know the exact position of the aircraft at all times.

Navigation is the art of determining geographic positions by means of observing identifiable objects on the ground, such as water towers giving the name of the town, railroad tracks, rivers, lakes, highways, and mountains.

Bombardier

Accurate and effective bombing is the ultimate purpose of your entire airplane and crew. Every other function is preparation to hit and destroy the target. That's your bombardier's job. The success or failure of the mission depends upon what he accomplishes during a short time on the bombing run.

The bombardier takes over the airplane for the run on the target. He is in absolute command. He will tell *you* what he wants done. Until he tells you "Bombs away," his word is law. Teamwork between pilot and bombardier is essential.

B-17s of the U.S. Eighth Air Force drop bombs high over Germany on December 24, 1944.

Radio Operator

Your radio operator will be required to give position reports every 20 minutes. He will assist the navigator by knowing the location of the aircraft. He will keep the command sets tuned and in good working order. The radio operator must understand all radio systems. He must also maintain a log of all outgoing and incoming messages.

Ammunition and ammo boxes

Gunners

You will rely on your gunners to protect the airplane from enemy aircraft. Each gunner must be familiar with all the gun turrets and other gun positions. They must be able to break down and reassemble any of the machine guns during flight, correct malfunctioning or jammed guns, and load ammunition into the ammo boxes. They should be trained in first aid.

CHAPTER 4

EVERY MAN TO HIS STATION

It wasn't easy to climb into a B-17 Flying Fortress or a B-24 Liberator wearing heavy fleece-lined jackets, pants, and boots and carrying a flak vest and a parachute.

B-17 Flying Fortress

On the B-17, the men entered through a hatch in the belly of the plane near the tail. Once aboard, each of the ten men went to his **station**.

In the cockpit, the copilot sat on the pilot's right. Below the cockpit and forward in the nose were the navigator and the bombardier. The radio operator's room, the **bomb bay**, and the waist-gunners' sections were in the rear of the plane.

B-17 crew positions

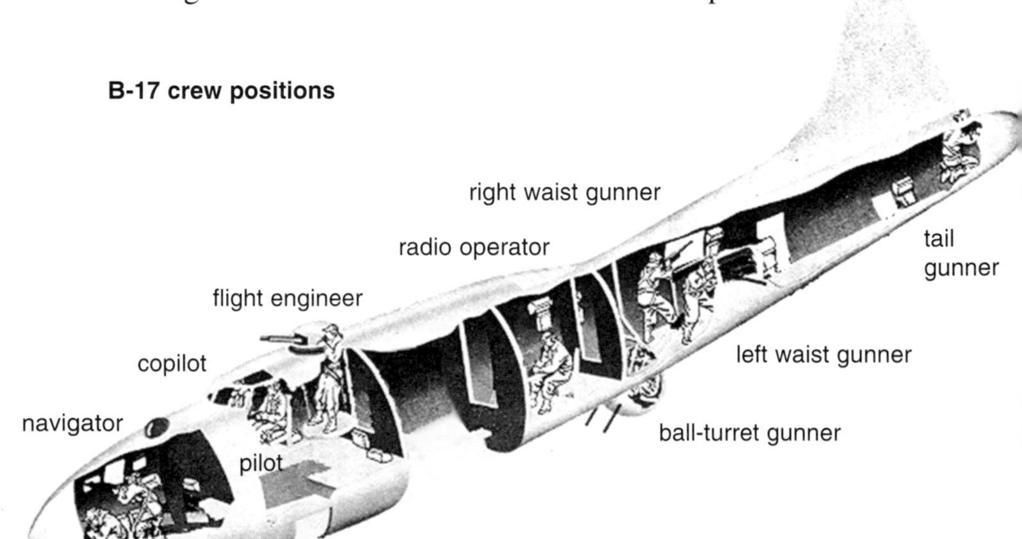

An army sentry guards new B-17F bombers at the Boeing airfield in 1942. They will be delivered to the army and the navy after they undergo flight tests.

The B-17 was heavily armed. A single .50-**caliber** machine gun was mounted in each of the two waist positions. Two .50-caliber machine guns were in both the tail turret and the ball turret. A .30-caliber machine gun was in the nose turret, and two .50 caliber guns were mounted in the top turret.

Plexiglas bubbles protected all of the turret gunners from the wind and extreme cold at high altitudes. Temperatures often dropped to -50°F.

The turrets were electrically operated and moved in any direction—up, down, and sideways. The upper turret also had a safety device to prevent the gunner from shooting off the tail of the airplane.

It was very lonely and cold inside the ball turret. The gunner often had to endure seven or eight hours in a cramped position with his knees almost touching his chin. He had to have a small **build** to crawl down into the turret.

The waist gunners, when not operating their guns, protected themselves from the wind and cold by closing the windows. But when firing the guns, the windows were open, no matter how cold it was.

B-24 Liberator

On B-24s, most of the crew entered through the open bomb bay doors and climbed up onto a narrow **catwalk** that ran through the center between the 500-pound bombs. The radio operator, pilot, and copilot worked their way forward to the **flight deck**. The waist and tail gunners moved toward the tail. The flight engineer stood just behind the pilot and copilot during takeoff. From there, he could read the engine and fuel gauges.

The bombardier, navigator, and nose-turret operators had to get down on their hands and knees and push their way into their cramped quarters in the nose of the plane. The bombardier had a small seat just behind the nose gunner in front of the Norden or Sperry bombsight. The navigator sat on a small **retractable** stool and worked at a table holding his maps.

SPERRY AND NORDEN BOMBSIGHTS

The Sperry and Norden bombsights were two of the most closely guarded secrets of the U.S. military during World War II. Even though both bombsights were used during the war, the Norden bombsight was the better known.

Invented by Carl Norden, the bombsight was used to determine the exact moment bombs had to be dropped to hit the target accurately. It was claimed to be accurate enough to hit a 100-foot circle from an altitude of 21,000 feet (4 miles).

Great precautions were taken to guard the secrecy of the bombsight. Armed guards loaded it onto an aircraft just before takeoff. When the plane landed back at base, the bombsight was immediately removed, again under armed guard, and **secured**. By war's end, over 45,000 bombardiers had been trained to use the bombsight. Each man swore under oath to protect its secrecy—if need be, with his life.

B-24 Liberator

The B-24 was quite similar to the B-17. The big difference was that in the B-17, the radio operator had a compartment all to himself. In the B-24, he sat at a small desk behind the copilot.

Like the B-17, the B-24 had a crew of ten men. There were four officers—pilot, copilot, navigator, and bombardier. The other six were enlisted men—radio operator, flight engineer, and four gunners. The radio operator and the flight engineer also manned guns.

The B-24 had two waist guns, a nose gun, a top turret, a ball turret, and a tail turret. The waist gunners' windows could not be closed. So they endured the bitter cold wind generated by traveling 300 miles per hour.

Unlike the ball-turret gunner on a B-17, the gunner on a B-24 had to have the turret lowered into position after he was inside. In case of an emergency, he had to rely on another crew member to "pump him up." In addition, his quarters were too confined for him to wear a parachute. For these reasons, his job was considered the most dangerous.

CHAPTER
5

"ALL FOR ONE, AND ONE FOR ALL"

When the ten men were selected to form a bomber crew, friendships were established that would last a lifetime. Facing extreme danger together molded a deep and lasting companionship that time could not erase. Each man relied upon the others to do their jobs completely, because doing otherwise meant possible death for the entire crew. From the time the crew formed until the last mission was flown, each man had absolute trust in the others. If, by chance, there was a "weak link" among them, the pilot could ask for that man to be transferred from the crew.

Once a crew was formed, it spent a month or two training as a group—learning to work together. A bomber was assigned. Usually the pilot gave the bomber a name, which he painted on the fuselage near the cockpit windows. Sometimes a picture went with the name.

Captain Wendell O. Pruitt, one of the leading pilots of the Fifteenth Air Force, talks with his crew chief.

Avengers flying in formation, 1942

Training took many forms. To practice bombing, the men used sandbags loaded with a small charge of dynamite and a **detonator** as bombs. The crews could test their accuracy with these.

Another training time was used for night flying. For practice, the planes flew at low altitudes. Then the gunners fired at targets on the ground.

The pilots and copilots practiced landings and takeoffs. Cross-country trips were scheduled so the navigators could practice charting routes.

Later in the training program, all the planes in the bomb group practiced **formation** flying. They duplicated the turns needed when entering a bomb run.

Simulated attacks by enemy planes also took place during training. A B-25, for instance, would come zooming in toward the bomber, and the gunners practiced aiming at it. No bullets were actually fired.

Finally, the important day the crews had been training for arrived. The pilots received orders for their crew and the assigned aircraft to fly to a combat zone. The orders were sealed so only the pilots knew where they were headed. The rest of the crew were told after the bombers had begun their flight overseas.

Planes took different routes to Europe depending upon whether they were joining the Eighth Air Force in England or the Fifteenth Air Force in Italy. Planes going to England flew to Gander Field in Newfoundland, Canada. From there, they crossed the Atlantic to England.

Crews flying to Italy took a much longer route. From Florida, they flew to Puerto Rico and then to Belem, Brazil. The next stops were in Fortaleza and Natal, Brazil. From Natal, the planes made the long night journey across the Atlantic to Africa. Several more stops were made crossing the Sahara desert to the Mediterranean coast. From there, the planes crossed the Mediterranean to Sicily and on to Italy. Most of the heavy bomber airfields were located around Grottaglie and Foggia in Italy.

Some crews were shipped over by boat. It was a long and somewhat dangerous journey. But by 1944, most of Germany's submarines were either sunk or disabled. The soldiers who went by boat were replacements for crews who had lost members.

CHAPTER 6

OFF WE GO INTO THE WILD BLUE YONDER

Just as it's getting light, the first engine coughs, sputters a little, and then roars into action. The propellers spin so fast that the individual blades are hard to see. Soon the other engines join in. Within five minutes, the roar of engines echoes from up and down the flight line.

The lead plane taxis to the head of the runway. It is three-quarters of the way down the runway when the next plane begins its takeoff. One after another, the planes move into position at the head of the runway and take off.

B-17 on the runway

Bombers flying in formation

The lead plane circles overhead, gaining altitude. One by one, the other planes join the formation. After 15 to 20 planes are airborne, the first **squadron** heads off toward the target. Then a second squadron forms and then a third and maybe a fourth, depending upon how many planes are flying the mission.

Inside each plane, the flight engineer reads aloud the data from several of the instruments on the panel in front of the pilot. The radio operator is in his seat, but none of his transmitters or receivers are on. Radio silence is maintained throughout the flight unless an emergency arises. Radio signals can alert the enemy.

The ball-turret gunner, the two waist gunners, and the tail gunner settle down in the waist compartment to listen to the cockpit intercom or just watch the scenery go by below. Because of the loud roar of the B-17's engines, conversation is almost impossible without shouting directly into one another's ears.

"Check your guns," comes the pilot's order over the intercom. The gunners go to their stations. Those who operate a turret test it first to make sure that it's operating correctly. Then the gunners fire a few rounds of ammunition to test the guns. Once completed, they return to the waist section and settle down again.

The plane reaches 10,000 feet. "Oxygen masks," the pilot orders. The men pull the masks over their faces and plug the flexible hose into the nearest oxygen outlet.

Not much later, the pilot tells the crew to man their stations. The plane has entered enemy territory. Silently the men go to their posts.

The temperature has dropped to below zero. All the gunners plug in their electric flying suits.

The men face three hours in their cramped turrets until they reach the target and another three hours on the return flight. They don't relax. They are constantly on the lookout for enemy planes. A few seconds of dozing can mean death for everyone aboard.

The tail gunner was responsible for sighting enemy aircraft approaching the plane from the rear. Waist gunners scanned the skies on both sides of the aircraft. The ball-turret gunner watched what was going on below the plane. He repeatedly swung his turret about so he could look in every direction.

Because the B-17s and B-24s flew at such a high altitude, any cloud cover was usually below the planes. The ball-turret operator usually spotted any ME-109s or Stuka dive bombers hiding in the clouds, ready to zoom up at the bomber.

STUKA DIVE BOMBER

During World War II, the German Ju-87 proved to be a powerful weapon. The name Stuka came from the German word *Sturzkampfflugzeug*, meaning "dive bomber." These planes were a vital part of the German battle plan. The planes carried wind whistles that would produce deathly screams as the planes dove toward their unfortunate target.

The top-turret gunner had a good view of the entire hemisphere above the plane. Like the ball-turret operator, he kept his turret in constant motion. The nose gunner had a limited view of the sky in front of the plane. The copilot, who had little to do except occasionally read aloud information from the many dials before him, also kept a close watch on the skies ahead.

The pilot had his hands full keeping the plane in tight formation with the rest of the squadron. By the time he brought the plane safely back to base, his arms ached from fighting the controls. Sometimes he found relief by turning the controls over to the copilot during the flight.

CHAPTER 7

BOMBS AWAY!

The navigator kept track of exactly where his plane was and what **heading** was needed to reach the target. He knew that when the plane approached the final bomb run, anything could happen. The plane could be damaged and drop out of the formation. If that happened, it was his job to direct the pilot back to base, using the best and safest route.

Things usually *did* happen the closer the formation came to the target. The enemy did everything it could to prevent the B-17s or B-24s from doing damage.

First, intense flak fire was aimed at the planes. The flak was set to burst at a preset altitude. When the shells burst, pieces of **shrapnel** exploded in every direction, easily penetrating a plane's thin fuselage. But it usually took a direct hit by a shell to bring down a bomber.

The pilot's and copilot's seats were protected underneath with armor. The other men had only their flak vests for protection, which some men didn't wear because there was no room in the turrets.

When the flak ceased, enemy fighter planes swooped in. They usually came from all directions, hoping to confuse the gunners. Coming at the bombers with the sun to their backs was an advantage for the enemy. **Evasive** maneuvers, such as **barrel rolling**, zigzagging, and changing altitudes quickly, were also used.

The turrets were programmed to allow for the speed of the bombers. The gunners had practiced many hours learning to aim *ahead* of moving objects. Every seventh or eighth bullet was a tracer, which glowed during its flight and showed the gunner how accurate his aim was. Most of the turrets had twin machine guns.

The navigator announces over the intercom that they are approaching the target. Now the bombardier takes over command of the plane. He tells the pilot the direction he wants the bomber to fly.

"Bomb bay doors open," he announces. The huge doors on the belly of the plane swing down. A bitter cold wind sweeps into the compartment where the waist gunners are firing their guns.

"Steady! Steady!" the bombardier tells the pilot. The plane must be level when he releases the bombs. The bombardier looks into the window of the bombsight. When he has the target in the **crosshairs**, he presses a switch.

"Bombs away!" he shouts.

The plane lifts suddenly from the loss of weight. The bomb bay doors close. The pilot resumes command and turns the plane toward the base—home.

ON A WING AND A PRAYER

This U.S. Air Force plane was damaged in a raid over Tokyo, Japan.

Not all planes reached the target, and some of those that did never made it back to base. Antiaircraft fire and enemy planes took their toll.

When planes took a direct hit, the chances of the crew bailing out were not good. Gravity **exerted** such terrific pressure when a plane dropped toward Earth that crew members not wearing safety belts were forced against the top of the plane and pinned there.

Gunners left their turrets, put on their parachutes, and found their way to an exit. The waist gunners had the best chance to jump free.

How fast a plane fell was determined by where the damage occurred. If the wings were shot off, the plane dropped like a stone. If the wings were intact, the plane swung back and forth as it dropped, much like a sheet of paper falling to the ground.

Officer trying to rescue pilot after a crash landing

If the damage was to an engine, the **hydraulic** system, or the tip of a wing or **stabilizer**, a skilled pilot might be able to get the plane back to base. The first thing he did was to instruct the crew to throw overboard anything that wasn't fastened down. It was important to make the plane as light as possible.

If the damage occurred before reaching the target, the bombardier released the bombs. If possible, the bombs were dropped over water. Often that wasn't the case. There were accounts of civilians killed and villages demolished by these bombs.

It was the flight engineer's job to assess any damage. He then determined if repairs could be made while the aircraft was in the air.

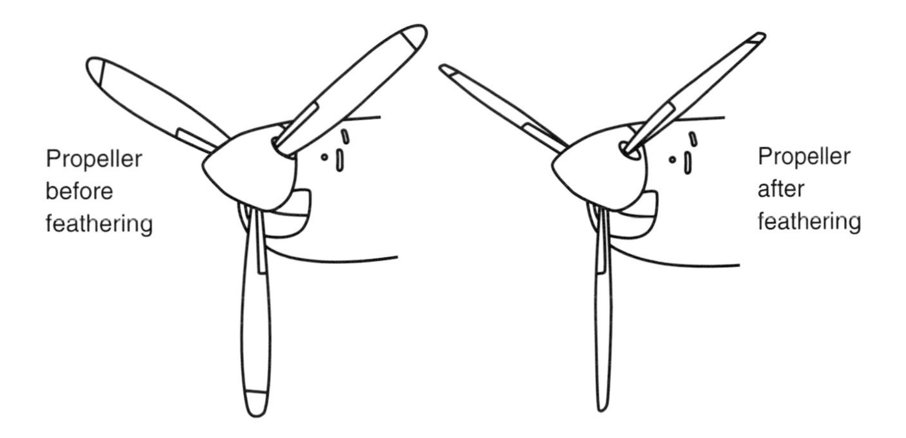

If an engine had been knocked out, the first thing the pilot did was to feather it. He did this by changing the angle of the propeller blades so there was less wind resistance. If he didn't do this, the plane would slow almost to a stop.

The pilot knew that he would gradually lose altitude. He made every effort to keep the plane from dropping too quickly. Sometimes the cables that controlled the **flaps** were cut by flak. Such damage made it very difficult for the pilot to control the plane.

The enemy watched for disabled planes like a tiger seeking wounded prey. To the Germans, a plane limping back home was an easy target. The crew prayed that there were no enemy aircraft in the area and that their disabled plane hadn't been spotted from the ground.

CHAPTER 9

IT HAPPENED TO ME

Many gunners kept journals of their missions. Here are two typical entries.

July 10, 1943

Everything went great until we began the bomb run. Like a bunch of angry bees, a swarm of ME-109s came at us from every direction. We were in the low squadron, and the ME-109s picked us out. Lieutenant Jayson had just announced over the intercom that the bomb bay doors were open. Suddenly, I felt the plane jolt. I was pitched forward and hit my head against the Plexiglas. I knew right away that one of our engines had been hit because we slowed down and began to drop. I didn't know it at the time, but the same shell that knocked out the engine also struck Lieutenant Billings, the pilot, in the head. Peterson, the copilot, took the controls and set the plane on **automatic pilot**. He checked to see what he could do for Billings, but it was too late. Peterson returned to the controls and took over command of the plane.

In the meantime, it was **chaos** back where I was. We managed to drop the bombs, although I don't think they hit anywhere near the target. As soon we were rid of the bombs, Peterson turned the plane toward base. That's when two fighters came at us, one from 2:00 high and one from 7:00 low.

2:00 HIGH!

When airmen looked at the sky, they imagined a clock in front of the plane. When one of the crew spotted an enemy aircraft, he called a time such as 2:00 or 7:00. Every airman aboard the plane knew where to look to find enemy aircraft. Today, people still use the clock reference when calling attention to a distant object.

"Seven o'clock low!" I yelled into the intercom for Bill in the ball turret. Little did I know then that he never heard it. A shell had severed the turret from the ship, and he had fallen to his death.

The two German planes scored some direct hits. One fighter sprayed a line of machine gun fire that ran from the tail turret along the fuselage to where the waist gunners were manning their guns. Pete was hit, but he was dead before I could reach him.

We finally got back to base with only a couple of hundred feet of altitude to spare. Peterson had to belly land because the wheels wouldn't come down. I guess that final burst of machine gun fire severed the hydraulic lines. Peterson had radioed ahead so a fire truck and **meat wagon** were waiting for us.

October 6, 1944

I'm writing this from **Stalag** 12 where I'm now a prisoner of war. The rest of my diary is back at base. Hopefully when they clean out my tent, they'll send it back to my parents with the rest of my stuff. Maybe not. Maybe there's classified stuff in the diary.

Anyway, this is how I got here. We were doing great until we left the target. I don't think anybody hit it because the Germans were burning smoke pots so the bombardiers couldn't see the target.

We weren't five minutes out of the bomb run when the flak became so thick you could cut it with a knife. We threw out lots of **chaff**, but it didn't seem to do any good. One B-24 behind us got a direct hit and went down like a rock. I didn't see any parachutes.

As soon as we ran out of the flak field, a flock of Focke-Wulfs came out of the clouds a mile or two behind us. I watched them grow closer through my optical gun sight.

FOCKE-WULF

The German Focke-Wulf ranked with the American P-51 Mustang as one of the best fighters of World War II. It entered combat the summer of 1941. From that time on, the Focke-Wulf kept even or ahead of Allied fighters in **kills**.

When the first enemy plane was within range, I let go three or four bursts. The fighter went into some evasive moves just as I fired. My shots went wild. The Focke-Wulf zoomed right over us—so close that for a second I could see the pilot's face. As he came by, he sprayed us with bullets. One of them glanced off the top of my turret and split it open.

Another enemy plane was right behind. When he was about 800 yards away, I gave him a few bursts. At 400 yards, I held the trigger down and gave him a continuous spray of bullets. I saw the **cowling** from his plane go flying into the air. He lost power and began to fall.

No more planes were coming in at me, but I knew that wasn't true for the other gun positions. All of a sudden, I felt a jolt. It seemed as if for a second the plane had stopped in midair.

I distinctly remember the conversation that followed. I'll never forget it as long as I live.

"Two engines on fire!" the pilot yelled to us over the intercom.

"Part of the left wing is gone," the waist gunner added.

"We're going down!" the pilot told us. "Bail out! Bail out! I'll try to hold her steady for a while."

I'd never parachuted, but I'd been given instructions as to what to do. I went to one of the waist hatches. The two waist gunners had already jumped. I ripped off my oxygen mask and helmet and then dove out the window like I was diving into a pool.

I cleared the wing. I knew I had to drop at least 10,000 feet. Then I'd be low enough to get out of the thin air. I counted to 20 instead of 10 and pulled the **ripcord**. Boy, was I glad to see that parachute billow over my head.

I made a good landing, got out of my harness, and rolled up the chute the best I could. I looked for a place to hide it.

That's when I saw Mike, one of the waist gunners. His parachute had caught in a tree. He was dangling about four or five feet above the ground. I left my parachute, found my pocketknife, and cut him down.

A while later, the other waist gunner joined us. We buried our chutes under a pile of leaves. But they weren't hidden very well.

We discovered three wide-eyed children from a nearby village watching us from some bushes. I didn't know what country we were in, so I kept my mouth shut. A few minutes later, two old men appeared. One of them had a shotgun. In German, he ordered us to follow him. None of us had brought our guns on the mission. We had no other choice but to follow.

We were turned over to the Gestapo, questioned, and brought here—to Stalag 12.

GESTAPO

The Gestapo was the German secret state police created by the government headed by Adolf Hitler. The agency was known for its cruel and ruthless treatment of those who opposed the Nazi government.

WHEN IT'S TIME TO BAIL OUT

Every airman was given detailed instructions of exactly what to do if it became necessary to bail out of a B-17 or a B-24.

When an emergency arose and it became necessary to bail out, there was no time for confusion or second-guessing. The procedure was automatic. When the order to abandon the airplane was given over the intercom, crew members snapped their parachutes onto the QAC harnesses and exited the plane.

QAC

The Quick Attachable Chest, or QAC, is a harness used for chest parachutes. The lightweight harness was worn over the airman's clothes. It had two turnbuckles to which the parachute could be attached very quickly.

Some airmen preferred to wear their parachutes at all times. Others waited until the pilot gave the signal to jump. If the plane was headed into water, the men removed the chutes since they would only be extra weight.

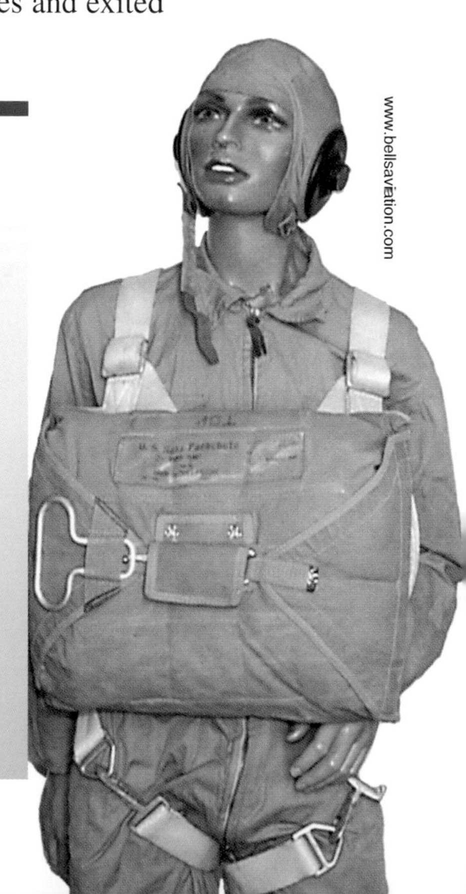

www.bellsaviation.com

Procedures for Bailing Out

- **Top-Turret Gunner:** His parachute was on the floor just forward of the bomb bay **bulkhead**. He exited first through the bomb bay.
- **Copilot:** His parachute was on the floor directly behind his seat. He exited second through the bomb bay.
- **Radio Operator:** His parachute was on the wall in the radio compartment. He exited third through the bomb bay.
- **Pilot:** His parachute was on the floor directly behind his seat. He was the fourth to exit through the bomb bay.
- **Navigator:** His parachute was on the bulkhead armor plating directly above the door in his compartment. He exited first through the front entrance door.
- **Bombardier:** His parachute was in the navigator's compartment. He exited second through the front entrance door.
- **Left Waist Gunner:** His parachute was on the wall near the left waist window. He was the first to exit through the main entrance door.
- **Right Waist Gunner:** His parachute was on the wall by the rear door. He exited second through the main entrance door.
- **Ball-Turret Gunner:** His parachute was on the right side of rear bulkhead of the radio compartment. He exited third through the main entrance door.
- **Tail Gunner:** His parachute was on the right wall immediately behind and above his escape hatch. He exited through a small emergency door in the rear.

CHAPTER 11

THE LUCKY ONES

Very seldom did all ten airmen get a chance to parachute from a plane that was going down. At the most, gunners on other planes only sighted three or four parachutes. Usually these were men who were closest to an escape hatch—the waist and tail gunners. The rest often went down with the plane.

Those who did manage to get out still were not "home free." Sometimes parachutes failed to open or opened with the lines tangled around the chute. On some occasions, the parachutes iced up passing through clouds, and the airmen would fall "like lead balloons." In places, the ground was so rough that the airmen were seriously injured when they landed even if the chutes operated properly. Some landed in water and drowned before they could free themselves from the chute harness.

A downed pilot waits for rescue in a life raft somewhere in the South Pacific.

If the men reached the ground safely, they still faced the risk of being caught. They became prisoners of war (POWs) unless they were lucky and landed in friendly territory.

In German-occupied countries, underground **resistance** groups helped downed airmen. They hid the airmen and helped them return to their bases.

But if airmen landed in Germany, they had little chance of not being found. No matter how cleverly they hid their tracks, the men were eventually caught by local citizens. The men were either shot or turned over to the Gestapo for interrogation and imprisonment. Some found themselves in one of Germany's stalags. They became *Kriegsgefangenens*, German POWs. Sometimes they escaped and found their way to a **neutral** country such as Switzerland.

If captured, the airmen were first questioned at a German interrogation center. According to international law, the only information they were required to give was their name, their rank, and the serial number engraved on their dog tags.

When the interrogations were over, the men were given Red Cross packages. These contained cigarettes, shaving equipment, and soap. The men were allowed to shower and shave.

Once at the prison camps, the men were assigned **barracks**. Each man received nine bed slats on which he placed a well-worn, lumpy mattress. Besides the limited amount of food the Germans provided, Red Cross packages of food arrived from time to time.

The one thing that concerned the prisoners most was not being able to let family and friends back home know that they were safe. They knew that telegrams would arrive that would say, "I regret to inform you that your son is missing in action." It meant that the soldier hadn't returned to base and the air force didn't know if he was alive or dead.

The International Red Cross in Geneva, Switzerland, attempted to keep track of all missing soldiers for both the Allies and the Axis countries. Red Cross workers notified POWs' families whenever they could. In addition, the Germans gave each POW a postcard. The POW was allowed to write a simple message that was sent to his family. It usually took weeks, sometimes months, before the postcard arrived at its destination.

INTERNATIONAL RED CROSS

Jean Henri Dunant, a Swiss citizen, created the Red Cross. After observing the effects of war, Dunant urged the formation of voluntary aid societies to provide relief for the victims of war. He also asked that service to military sick and wounded be neutral. The result was the formation of the organization in 1863 that became known as the Red Cross.

An agreement that was signed in 1864 by 16 nations provided for the humane treatment of the wounded. It also assured that medical personnel in the armed forces and the civilians who voluntarily assisted them be neutral in their treatment of the wounded and that an international emblem be used to mark medical personnel and supplies. In honor of Dunant's nationality, a red cross on a white background—the Swiss flag with colors reversed—was chosen as the symbol for the new organization.

After families knew that their sons were being held in POW camps, they could send packages. One package for each POW was permitted every 60 days. Families were warned not to use any stickers or write anything on the packages that contained patriotic messages or anti-German slogans. Still not all the packages reached the POWs, especially near the end of the war when there was a severe food shortage in Germany.

All U.S. soldiers who were caught and imprisoned had been taught that it was their duty to make every effort to escape. A captured U.S. officer was assigned to each enlisted men's barracks. He was responsible for their safety and well-being. Secretly, however, he worked with the men to plan escapes and, if possible, to **sabotage** German installations and send critical information back to the Allies.

U.S. soldiers after escaping from a POW camp at Limburg, Germany

CHAPTER
12

IN THE "DRINK"

If a plane became disabled and went down over water, the pilot warned the crew that he was about to ditch the plane. Each crew member was then required to acknowledge that he heard the warning. Acknowledgements were given in a specific order—copilot, navigator, bombardier, flight engineer, radio operator, ball-turret gunner, right waist gunner, left waist gunner, and tail gunner. As soon as acknowledgements were made, crew members removed their parachutes and flying boots and loosened their collars. They removed their oxygen masks once the plane dropped below 12,000 feet.

Crew members prepared for the **impact**. They sat on the floor, bent forward, and wrapped their arms about their heads. Two impacts were felt. The first was a mild jolt when the tail struck the water. The second one, when the nose hit, was severe.

As soon as the plane came to a stop on the water, the crew released the life rafts. Extreme care was taken to make sure that none of the rafts were punctured by sharp edges on the wings as they were shoved into the water. Care was taken to make sure that the rafts were tied together. Injured men were removed first.

Each man made sure that his life vest fit through the escape hatch before he inflated it. After every crew member was safely in a raft, the pilot took an inventory of how much food and water was available. Strict **rationing**, controlled by the pilot, was maintained. Flares were used only when there was a reasonable chance they would be seen by a passing ship or aircraft.

CHAPTER 13

BACK TO BASE

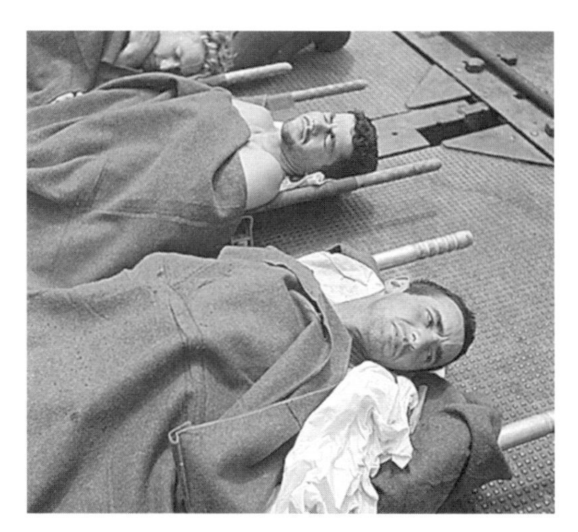

Men wounded in Okinawa await transfer to a hospital ship.

Landing

Planes with wounded aboard land first while the remaining planes circle overhead. Ambulances wait. The wounded men are placed on stretchers and carried to the ambulance. They're rushed to the base hospital where doctors have prepared for them.

Next to land are the damaged planes and those running low on fuel. Fire trucks stand by.

One plane can't lower its landing gear. The pilot is forced to belly land. Sparks spew out from the fuselage as the plane strikes the metal grids of the runway. The pilot works frantically to keep the plane from turning over or barreling off the runway.

He finally stops right at the end of the runway. A fire breaks out under the right wing. The crew exits quickly, leaving everything behind. They scatter, getting as far away from the plane as possible.

Suddenly flames engulf the aircraft. A few seconds later, the plane explodes. Pieces of metal and Plexiglas shower down hundreds of yards away. The fire trucks pull up as close as they dare and spray the flames with foam.

In the meantime, the remaining planes land on what's left of the runway. A few cannot stop quickly enough to avoid hitting the burning wreckage and are forced to swerve to the right or left. Two of them overturn. No one aboard is seriously injured.

Debriefing

All gunners and officers who have not been injured are required to attend a **debriefing**. It is held in the same building where the men met that morning. The **brass** who planned the mission need to know how successful it was. They also want to know what the pilots, the navigators, the bombardiers, and the gunners saw. How accurate was the bombing? How many bombs missed the target? Did anyone witness any explosions at or near the target areas? How many of the target buildings were on fire?

They need to know about losses too. How many lives were lost? How many planes went down and at what point in the mission were they hit? How many parachutes were seen? From which planes?

Enemy strength is another concern. How thick was the flak? Was it on target? From what location was it coming? How many enemy fighters attacked? How many were destroyed? What types of aircraft were they?

An aide sits at a desk taking notes of everything that is said. A few of the planes were equipped with cameras. Later, the brass will hold a meeting and discuss this information. It will help them plan the future missions.

Time to Relax

The debriefing is over. The officers head straight for the officers' club and the gunners to the enlisted men's club. There are drinks, music, and dancing.

The veteran gunners talk. New crews, who have just arrived from the States, listen attentively. They ask questions. They want to know what it's like to fly a mission. They want to know which are the milk runs and which are not.

The veterans don't boast. They give the **greenhorns** the facts just as they are. They tell them about some of the missions they've been on—the easy ones *and* the hard ones. They remember when they, too, were greenhorns and how they felt before that first mission. They remember the butterflies in their stomachs, the sleepless nights, and the nightmares.

Some of the men prefer to stay in their tents, reading or writing letters home. A single bulb hanging from the center pole provides light. A few tents have radios, and the men listen to the news broadcasts from Britain or to the latest hit songs.

Some nights, the USO holds shows featuring celebrities from back home. The shows are staged on the **tarmac**. The men sit on the ground. A makeshift stage is erected for the entertainers.

The gunners do everything they can to take their mind off the events of the day. They try to forget that tomorrow or the next day or even the one after, they will have to go through it all again. Only maybe the next time, they won't be so lucky.

UNITED SERVICE ORGANIZATIONS

In 1940, President Franklin D. Roosevelt challenged six private organizations—the YMCA, the YWCA, the National Catholic Community Service, the National Jewish Welfare Board, the Traveler's Aid Association, and the Salvation Army—to handle the on-leave recreation needs of the members of the armed forces. The six organizations pooled their resources, and the United Service Organizations (USO) was born.

The goal of the USO was to provide a place for drafted soldiers to be entertained without getting into trouble. The first USO centers were in railroad sleeping cars, barns, museums, and churches in the States.

As the United States plunged into World War II, Hollywood wanted to do its part. Actors, who usually played in fancy theaters or on the "big screen," now found themselves on the "Victory Circuit." They traveled to remote places and performed on makeshift stages in the blistering sun and in the freezing cold.

Soon, the USO became famous for its lineup of Hollywood's greatest talent performing for the troops in every World War II theater of battle. These all-stars included Bob Hope, the Andrews Sisters, Clark Gable, Mickey Rooney, James Stewart, Laurel and Hardy, Glenn Miller, Benny Goodman, Bing Crosby, Gary Cooper, James Cagney, Fred Astaire, Humphrey Bogart, and Marlene Dietrich. Just the presence of these stars brought sick, lonely, and wounded servicemen a slice of home.

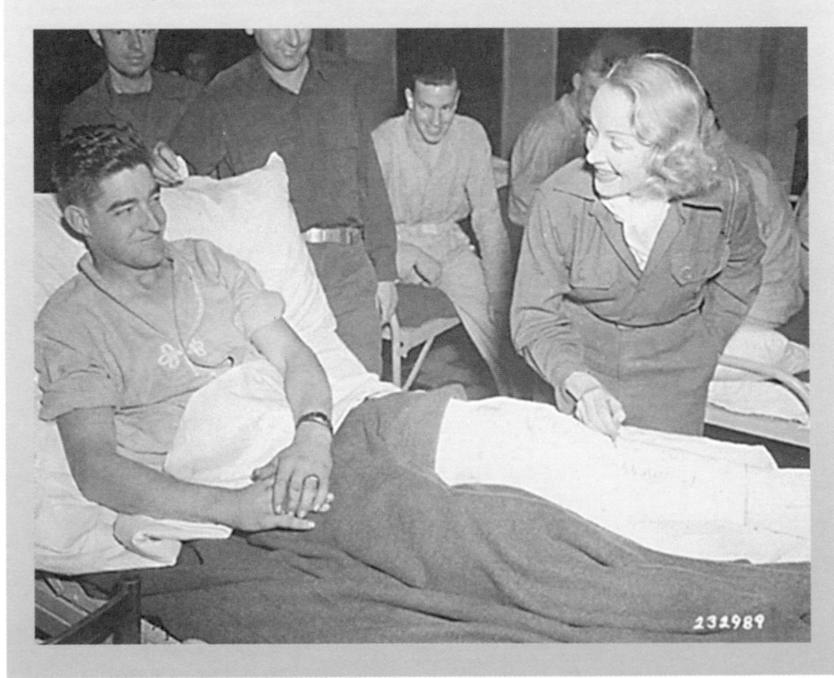

Marlene Dietrich authographs the cast of a wounded soldier.

CHAPTER 14

WHEN SKIES ARE GRAY

Life on the Base

The crews in Italy lived in tents. The six enlisted men of a crew shared one tent, and the four officers shared another. Many crews worked to improve their living conditions.

Whenever it rained hard, water would run through the tents and turn the floors into mud. To remedy this, old crates were broken apart, and the wood was used to build floors.

Halves of empty 50-gallon gasoline drums served as stoves. An opening was cut in the front. For fuel, gasoline was stored in back of the tent and fed into the stove through tubes taken from **demolished** aircraft. The end of the tube was **crimped** so only a drop or two of gas dripped into the fuel box at a time. Occasionally, this crude device had terrible results. The tent and everything in it blew up.

Some crew members found pets—a dog usually. After a while, the dog became the squadron's pet. It ate in the mess hall and slept on whichever cot it preferred. Somehow the dog knew when a crew didn't come back. It would go to the empty tent and "cry."

Two main air forces from the United States were based in the European theater of operations—the Eighth in England and the Fifteenth in Italy. England was noted for its rainy weather. In Italy, it also rained frequently during the winter months.

Free Time

Until the last year of the war when radar bombing was introduced, all bombing was done by eyesight. Sight bombing required that the bombardier had visual contact with the target. When it rained or when there was cloud cover, missions were not scheduled or they were cancelled at the last moment. On these days, combat crews had a holiday, or some free time.

Some airmen signed out a jeep and traveled to see the countryside. Others visited the closest town. In England, they went to the local pubs, saw a movie, met a British family, visited a museum or historical site, or perhaps dated a local girl. In Italy where there was a language barrier, becoming friends with the locals was more difficult.

Those who stayed on the air base wrote letters to family and friends back home, played cards, read books, wrote in their journals, listened to the radio, or stayed in the sack all day.

Furloughs

After a specified number of missions, crew members were eligible for a **furlough**. In Italy, the men often went to the Isle of Capri. They rented boats and explored the underwater **caverns** of the Blue Grotto. They slept in the luxury of hotel rooms where they were waited on hand and foot. It was a time for them to relax and forget the missions and dangers that lay ahead.

CHAPTER
15

FIGHTER ESCORTS

B-17 bomber

Early in the war, the United States and its allies had no fighters that could accompany the bombers on long missions. Therefore, even the heavily armed B-17s, B-24s, and the British Lancasters and Wellingtons were no match for the well-trained Luftwaffe, the German air force, pilots. The British Spitfire and the American Lockheed P-38 and Republic P-47 Thunderbolt were limited-range fighters. They couldn't carry enough fuel to escort bombers for long missions.

Spitfire

P-51 Mustangs

Later in the war, the American P-51 Mustang was developed. It could fly decp into Germany to escort and protect the bombers. It carried sufficient fuel to make the return flight. The Mustang's maximum speed was 445 miles per hour at 25,000 feet. It weighed 7125 pounds. Mounted on its wings were six .50-caliber machine guns. Each Mustang could carry two 500-pound bombs.

These fighters flew at a greater speed than the bombers. When they were not engaged in fighting enemy attack planes, they weaved back and forth overhead. No other combat plane, Allied or German, could fly as high or go as far as the Mustangs. They fought with more enemy planes and had to their credit more kills than any other Allied aircraft.

THE TUSKEGEE AIRMEN

During World War II, one of the most distinguished fighter groups of the war was the 332nd Fighter Group—the Tuskegee Airmen. These African American pilots were relentless in their defense of the bombers that they were assigned to escort and protect. Many of the pilots sacrificed their lives.

After a time, the 332nd Fighter Group's reputation grew. B-17, B-24, and other bomber crews requested them over other escorts. They became known as the Red Tails because the tails of their planes were painted red.

Tuskegee pilot
Howard A. Wooten

The short-range P-38s and the Thunderbolts would first escort bombers flying from England. The Mustangs would leave about an hour later and catch up to the bombers. The P-38s and Thunderbolts would head back to home base, and the Mustangs would finish escorting the bombers for the remainder of the mission.

CHAPTER 16

TWO TRAITORS

Axis Sally

In the European theater of operations, the airmen enjoyed listening to Axis Sally on the radio because she played all the songs that were popular back home. Unfornately, she also used **propaganda**.

"Hey, you there," she would say. "Yes, I'm talking to you guys who risk your neck every day flying those planes. Know who's getting cozy with your girl back home? Yeah, that's right. Some 4-F guy. By the time you get back, she'll have forgotten all about you. So why don't you just quit and go back to her now?"

4-F RATING

Some men who were drafted by the army were rated 4-F. The 4-F rating meant that these men were unable to serve in the armed forces because of physical or mental health reasons.

Axis Sally was born in Portland, Maine, and attended Ohio Wesleyan College. Her real name was Mildred Elizabeth Gillars. She left college in 1922. She worked at various jobs until 1935. She then moved to Germany where she became an English teacher.

After the war broke out in 1939, Gillars began broadcasting propaganda for Germany from a radio studio in Tunis, Tunisia. She often surprised Allied commanders by broadcasting information that was top secret.

When the Allies took command of North Africa from the Germans, Gillars moved back to Germany. From there, she continued to broadcast propaganda programs to British and American servicemen until the end of the war.

In 1949, Gillars was convicted of treason and sentenced to 30 years in prison. She served 12 years in a United States prison and then was released. She finished her studies at Ohio Wesleyan and taught school in Columbus, Ohio. She died in 1988.

Mildred Gillars (Axis Sally) walking to a jail van after her conviction of treason

Tokyo Rose

In the Pacific theater of operations, another traitor broadcast propaganda for the Japanese. Iva Ikuko Toguri, known as Tokyo Rose, was born in a suburb of Los Angeles. After she graduated from the University of California in 1941, she moved to Japan to take care of a sick aunt. She was trapped in Japan when the Japanese bombed Pearl Harbor and the United States declared war.

A prison photo of Iva Ikuko Toguri (Tokyo Rose)

Being a U.S. citizen, she was looked upon with suspicion by the authorities. Her knowledge of both English and Japanese and her ability to type enabled her to get a job with a Japanese news agency. She also held a part-time job at a broadcast studio. After a time, she was asked to read prepared scripts, which would be broadcast to Australian, British, and American servicemen. She refused but was forced to do so by the Japanese military colonel in charge of the radio station. Though she used the name Orphan Ann, the Allied servicemen knew her as Tokyo Rose.

After the war, Toguri was sentenced to ten years in prison and fined $10,000. She claimed innocence her entire life. In the 1970s, new information and testimony from former American POWs led to a complete pardon in 1977 by President Gerald Ford.

THE END, AT LAST!

Pilots celebrating victory

By spring 1945, the Allies were closing in on Berlin, the capital of Germany. On the afternoon of April 30, German Leader Adolf Hitler committed suicide in his **bunker**. On May 8, Germany surrendered.

When the news reached the airmen in England and Italy, there was a continuous celebration all day and into the night. "It was like a heavy load was taken off my chest," said a ball-turret gunner on a B-17. "It was like I was suddenly let out of jail."

"I had just finished my eighteenth mission," Sidney, a waist gunner remarked. "I was to the point where I couldn't sleep nights anymore because as soon as I'd get to sleep I'd have terrible nightmares. The plane would blow up. Or I would go down and couldn't get out. I'd wake up. I'd try to get back to sleep, but I couldn't. I was so tired the next day I couldn't keep my eyes open. That wasn't fair to the rest of my crew. I was ready to get grounded. When I heard the war was over, I was so happy, believe it or not, I cried. What a relief! It's been a long war!"

For the British, the war had lasted almost six years. For the Americans, it lasted four. During that time, the army air force trained 193,000 pilots, 50,000 navigators, and 45,000 bombardiers. But the number of aerial gunners who were trained exceeded the pilots, navigators, and bombardiers together. Flexible gunnery schools turned out 297,000 gunners.

Accounts of World War II emphasized the great battles fought by the navy, by the marines, and by the infantry. The air force received little of the recognition it deserved. It lost close to 23,000 planes and 88,000 airmen. It dropped 2 million tons of bombs and downed 40,000 enemy planes.

Oil refineries, ammunition dumps, steel plants, ball bearing factories, railroads, and supply routes were all destroyed by these men—these "boys." They flew at high altitudes where temperatures fell to -50°F and life could only be sustained with the aid of oxygen masks. They flew where heavy antiaircraft guns and enemy fighter planes downed an average of one out of every ten planes per mission.

These aerial gunners were the unsung heroes of World War II.

GLOSSARY

altitude height above Earth's surface

attention formal way of standing used by members of the armed forces. Feet are together, eyes are straight ahead, and arms are straight at the sides.

automatic pilot control in the steering system of an aircraft that can be set to keep the plane on a steady course

bail out to escape from a plane that is in danger of crashing by making a parachute jump

barracks building that houses military people

barrel rolling flight maneuver in which an aircraft makes one complete sideways revolution

bomb bay compartment on a bomber in which the bombs are carried

brass high-ranking officers in the military

briefing meeting held to provide information

build physical structure, shape, and size of a person

bulkhead partition inside an aircraft

bunker underground shelter

caliber outside diameter of a bullet or shell

catwalk narrow, raised walkway

cavern large underground cave or a large chamber in a series of caves

chaff glass fibers or silvered nylon filaments released into the air as an antiradar measure

chaos state of complete disorder and confusion

classified available only to those certain people who have been cleared, or okayed, by the government. The basic categories of classified information are confidential, secret, and top secret.

close-order drill formation (see separate glossary entry) or movement that is conducted at close range

cowling metal covering for an aircraft engine

crimp pinch to almost closed

crosshair fine line in the focus of the eyepiece of a sighting instrument that's used as a reference line

debriefing meeting after a mission has ended when reports are given about what happened

deflect to cause a change of course by blocking something

demolished damaged so badly it can't be repaired

detonator device used to make a bomb or a quantity of explosives explode

ditch to land an aircraft on water in an emergency

dog tags two metal identification tags on a chain, worn around the neck by a member of the military

draft to select someone for required military service

efficiency ability to do something well or achieve a desired result without wasted energy or effort

emplacement position that is specially prepared for a large gun or group of guns

enlist to join a branch of the armed forces

escort one or more fighter aircraft that accompanies and provides protection for a larger aircraft that is more likely to be attacked

evasive intended to avoid an attack

exert to apply with power

flak relating to antiaircraft fire directed from the ground

flap narrow, movable surface attached to the rear edge of an aircraft wing that is used to create lift or drag

flight deck compartment at the front of an airplane where the pilot, copilot, and flight engineer are found

formation precise arrangement of a group for a particular purpose

furlough leave of absence from duty for a military person

fuselage airplane's body without the wings

GI government issued; provided by the armed forces for the use of its members

greenhorn newcomer with little or no experience

hardstand hard surface on which aircraft are parked

heading direction in which an aircraft is traveling

hydraulic relating to the pressure that is transmitted when a quantity of liquid is forced through a small tube to make something such as flaps (see separate glossary entry) work

impact force with which one object hits another

kill slang meaning "enemy plane destroyed"

marshaling yard area occupied by many parallel railroad tracks where railroad cars are held until they are made into trains

meat wagon slang meaning "ambulance"

mess hall building where a group of people, especially members of the armed forces, eat their meals together

milk run routine, uneventful trip or sortie (see separate glossary entry)

munitions dump place where large supplies of arms and ammunition are held

neutral not belonging to, favoring, or assisting any side in a war

Plexiglas trademark for a tough, transparent acrylic plastic that can be used in place of glass

propaganda information put out by an organization or government to spread and promote a policy, idea, doctrine, or cause. The information is often altered or false.

rationing	act of controlling the amount of supplies that are used
resistance	relating to an illegal secret organization that fights for national freedom against an occupying power
restricted	intended only for people who have been cleared, or okayed
retractable	able to be drawn in from an extended position
rigorous	extremely precise, difficult, and formal
ripcord	cord that is pulled to open a parachute
sabotage	to damage, destroy, or disrupt something purposely, especially during a war
sack	slang word meaning "bed"
secure	to guard and provide protection against attack or theft
shrapnel	metal balls or fragments that are scattered when a shell, bomb, or bullet explodes
simulated	faked but designed to seem real
sortie	mission flown by a combat aircraft
squadron	group of planes consisting of two or more aircraft that have the same mission
stabilizer	device in the tail assembly of an airplane that keeps an aircraft aligned with the direction of flight
stalag	German POW (prisoner of war) camp in World War II
station	place where a military person is sent to carry out his or her duties
tarmac	runway
transcribe	to write something out in full from a code
turret	a dome projecting from the fuselage (see separate glossary entry) of an aircraft containing one or more guns and a gun crew
unauthorized	not having permission to be somewhere

INDEX